A Journey through Infinity

Soul Food Poems

authorHOUSE®

AuthorHouse™
1663 Liberty Drive
Bloomington, IN 47403
www.authorhouse.com
Phone: 1-800-839-8640

Published by AuthorHouse 3/22/2013

ISBN: 978-1-4817-3278-9 (sc)
ISBN: 978-1-4817-3277-2 (e)

Library of Congress Control Number: 2013905221

Any people depicted in stock imagery provided by Thinkstock are models, and such images are being used for illustrative purposes only. Certain stock imagery © Thinkstock.

This book is printed on acid-free paper.

Table of Contents

This book is dedicated to all those poets that came before me, and to all those who will come after me. I would like to thank my aunt Olivia A. Fletcher for encouraging me to keep writing. To my editor, Denise Fountain, thanks for helping me with my books... you are truly a great friend! To my nieces and nephews, Auntie Dawn loves you all! Last but definitely not least, to my baby girl Anansa, Mommy does it all for you the love of my life!

In loving memory of Barbara L. Hughes and Myrtle Brents
Miss you both dearly!

Letter to a Good Man

There are quite a few women
Who have completely given up on finding a good man
They have become frustrated and weary tryin to understand...
Understand why it is they keep running across men
Who truly aren't worthy of their love and affection
They are desperately looking for what they consider their
     mirrored reflection
They have yet to realize that they are looking too hard for love
And that they are tryin to get it from every man they meet
They don't realize that they already need to be whole
And that a man can't make them complete
You see, there are plenty of good men still walking around,
But the bad ones are giving you all a bad name
But we as women need to stop messing over the good men by
     playin silly games
I've seen you in action so I know what you are capable of
I admire your strength and your ability to show true love
This is my letter to a good man
I applaud you my husband, my lover, my friend
This is my letter to you
For not letting stereotypes or society hold you back,
And for you starting your own trend
This is my letter to you to show you that I appreciate every little
     thing you do
I love the fire I see in you;
To excel at being a good man, father and role model to our seeds
You feed their needs as you rear this new breed
Teachin ya son how to be a good man and teachin ya daughters

how not to settle for the Guy who wants to take advantage
    of her innocence
Teachin them that when they do wrong, they will have to suffer
    the consequence
This is my letter to you, a good man
Even though we may not always agree,
I know you are still doing the very best you can
You are not as rare as some women would have it seem,
I'm glad I've found you and I will always be on your team
I will always assist your every play; I will always be your #1 fan
This is my letter to you, A Good Man

Mr. DJ

I sit watching you as you fall into a zone
Your mind is focused
Your thoughts remain on movin the crowd
You become the music
You have formed a bond
Every emotion within you
You release through scratchin' and mixin'
You blend beats that keeps the crowd on its feet
I watch you with excitement
As your hands glide over each piece of vinyl
I become envious
Wishing I was that record your fingers ran across
But at the same time
I enjoy the passion I see on your face
While you become the life of the party
Commanding the crowd with each song you play
Keepin' them crunk or even mellow
They become captivated by you
Like fiends they await the next song
You become their high
Their drug of choice
As you spin hit after hit
You become elated
Even addicted yourself
To the power you posses over the crowd
I watch you
As you transform into this mega mixin' beast
As you unleash

Perfectly blended beats
As you hypnotize the crowd
Song
After
Song
They
Move
Just
For
You
They need you
To make them sweat

They need you
For their nightly high
They need you
To keep their night alive
Mr. DJ
The party starter
The crowd pleaser
The musical drug pusher
The beat maker
Keep the party going
Mr. DJ

Sometimes I Feel

Sometimes I feel, like a motherless child
Sometimes I feel, like a motherless child

I sit in the distance thinkin' this life isn't real
Spinnin' in place
Going nowhere
Like a car without wheels

I try to reboot this scene
Control, Alt, Delete
My life has become frozen
Control, Alt, Delete
Damn, I'm stuck on this screen

Sometimes I feel, like a motherless child
Sometimes I feel, like a motherless child

I sit in corners like an aborted fetus
Regurgitatin' my life back
To a time when it was just us

Perfection in my life seems so farfetched
Memories of happiness
In my mentals
Have become permanently etched

Sometimes I feel, like a motherless child
Sometimes I feel, like a motherless child

Sometimes I feel
Like happiness is on pause
Like all truths contain flaws
Like deception is on the rise
Like to fit in, you have to wear a disguise

Sometimes I feel, like a motherless child
Sometimes I feel, like a motherless child

Sometimes I feel
Like 10 million children in an orphanage
Like innocent victims being held hostage
Like flyin into a violent rage
Like a bird with no wings, livin in a cage

I try to reboot this scene
Control, Alt, Delete
This life has become frozen
Control, Alt, Delete
Damn, we are all still stuck on this screen

Sometimes
We
All
Feel like
Motherless
Children

The Poet vs. The Rapper

Some might say that a poet and a rapper are one in the same
But I think there's a huge difference between the 2
The Poet vs. The Rapper
Their differences are in plain view

Poets spit words and weave literary prose from their heart
Rappers spit fairytales while tryin to obtain platinum and gold
Poets open up and show you the depths of their soul
Rappers talk about bling, money, clothes and hoes
Poets let you explore your own emotions from their point of view
Rappers talk about shit they've never even been through

The Poet vs. The Rapper
Their differences are in plain view

Now, don't get me wrong
Not all rappers are stuck on that same materialistic bullshit
Some of them actually have something to say, an opinion to give
Talkin' about real life issues
Talkin' about political issues
Talkin' about social issues

The Poet vs. The Rapper
Their differences are in plain view

A majority of today's rappers though, have lost the essence of
    true hip hop

They keep their focus on gettin the most money, the most cars
    and the most bling
When in reality, none of that shit means a thing

The Poet vs. The Rapper
Their differences are in plain view

Meanwhile, Poets focus on their feelings, reality and life
Poets tell stories that pierce your soul deeper than any knife
Poets, we don't do what we do to try to get rich
We do what we do for love of this

For the love words
For the love of emotions

For the love verbs
For the love of romantic notions
We do what we do to release our pain
We don't do this for recognition or street fame
We do what we do to touch the world
We do what we do to reach lost boys and girls

Rappers may have a few good years on the scene
Real good rappers come far and few in between
But Poets will be weaving literary prose from now 'til the hereafter
Their differences are in plain view
The Poet vs. The Rapper

A *work in progress*/Under Construction

I am a work in progress
My life is still under construction
Each morning when I wake, I try to focus on the good in life
I try not to judge others
I try to speak words of kindness
I try to remember that we are all made in His likeness

Sometimes, I fall short
Sometimes, I stray away from His word
Sometimes, the devil finds his way in
Sometimes I think it's too hard to walk the walk
And talk the talk

But when I stray too far, I feel Him bringing me back
I hear Him speakin' to my soul
I remember that no one is perfect

We are all at different places in our walk with Him
So, I don't fret too long over the choices I've made
Instead, I learn from them

I remember that we are all His children
That all our lives are still under construction
And that because of Him, we are all special

So, when I feel like others are judging me
Persecuting me
Or turning their noses up at me

I just remind myself
That I am a work in progress
That He is not finished with me yet
That they cannot lead me into destruction
'Cause my life is still under His construction

Desperate, The Entertainer

I arrived on the set today
Lookin' extra sexy
If I do say so myself, and I do
I know this part is mine
I plan on doing whatever it takes

I see the stars coming my way
Lookin' at all the girls
But truthfully, none of them compare to me

My body is bangin'
And no man can resist
My big brown eyes
My little waist
My Double D's
Or my perfectly round ass

As the stars get closer
I get nervous for only a second
As they get close enough to hear only my voice
I whisper softly, "I'll let you hit to be in your video"

See, I know that's what it takes
To make it in the industry
Girls come from all around the world
To try to be featured in these videos
So, I'm not ashamed of what I do
I know that closed mouths don't get fed

My Mom always said
"You've got to use what you've got, to get what you want"
Over the years, I've followed her advice
And have been the main girl in plenty of videos

Some of the other chicks get mad 'cause I got picked
But hey, they should know the rules before they try to play the
    game
Yeah, some of the guys have called me sluts and hoes
But they're just jealous
And that's what I do know

I've got to make sure my future is set
So I don't worry about what I might grow to regret
I'm all about gettin ahead
While the Miss Goody Goody's sit around and bitch instead

They better step their game up
And stop being labeled as complainers
'Cause I'm comin for the #1 spot
So watch out for me
Desperate, The Entertainer!

Betrayed

You have given up on me
You say my strength is too much for you
You say that I have way too much attitude
And for this, I feel betrayed

You say you can no longer love me
You say that my mind and strength make me unattractive
You say I have too much mouth
And for this, I feel betrayed

You say only others can give you what you need
You say you can never see yourself with me again
You say that even your mother has too much attitude
And for this, I feel betrayed

You say I don't know how to have your back
You say I emasculate you
You say I am not passive enough for you
And for this, I feel betrayed

You see I feel betrayed because it was I that nourished your
     growth
It was I that wrapped you in my bosom of security
It was I that you first adored
It was I that was there for you during your struggle to the top
It was I that understood your daily triumphs

And now it is I that you turn your back on?

You forgot who helped you out of the ghetto
Steered you away from drugs
Stopped you from the unnecessary hustling
And it was I that showed you that together we could make it
    through anything

My strength you once needed
My love you once needed
And now, you toss me away like yesterday's news
Despite my blues, my soul you chose to bruise
And say that I am to blame
You say that for my strength, I should be ashamed

You tell me my ways are a curse
And now, you put her first?
You say that women of color are no longer what you desire
You say that now it's her you admire?

If love is what you were truly searching for then that I can
    accept
But believe me your true reasons….you will surely regret
You have betrayed all those who look like me
Those who are strong like me
And whose support you will one day need

You have given up on me
You say my strength is too much for you
You say that I have way too much attitude
And for this, I feel betrayed

You say you can no longer love me
You say that my mind and strength make me unattractive
You say I have too much mouth
And for this, I feel betrayed

You say only other's can give you what you need

You say you can never see yourself with me again
You say that even your mother has too much attitude
And for this, I feel betrayed

You say I don't know how to have your back
You say I emasculate you
You say I am not passive enough for you
And for this, I feel betrayed

I am the Magnificent

The best poet in my eyes
Is Me
'Cause I am only comparin
My magnificence to me

My own ability to create lyrical masterpieces
To weave stories in poetic prose
To spin verbs
Like no one has ever heard

I am the best at being me
And I don't take anything from anyone else poetically
I revel in my fellow poets' magnificence
Each time we share our poetry
It just builds up the magnificence in me

I am the magnificent in my eyes
'Cause I never hold myself to anyone else's expectations
Other than my own
My work is unique in a sense
That it comes from me

It dwells within my inner being
Opening up my mind, allowin my feelings to be free
It's my ability to share my past hurts, and pains
Hopin that through my words, others will gain
Some sense of understandin', and will be able to relate
My magnificence spews out onto pages and stages where I recite

I've had fellow poets compare their work to mine
And they seem to think their work is not as good as mine
So, I've had to break it down for them
To tell them they are right
Their work is not as good as mine
It's as good as theirs
I've had to tell them
Never to compare their work to anyone else's
Never to compare their thoughts, their emotions, or their
    experiences
That they are magnificent in their own right

As I am magnificent in my own right
I am the best poet I will ever be
But as I grow
So will my flows
And my magnificence
Will know no bounds
As I continue to astound
MYSELF

I am the Magnificent!

For my Daughter

Excitement filled my heart
The day the doctor said
It's a girl

I prayed for you
And finally
You came into my world

So many things to teach you
So many things I want you to learn
Things I hope you can pass on
When it's finally your turn

Pretty dresses and bows
No longer am I a little girl
Playing dress up
My dreams have finally
Come true

I sat for hours
Watching you
As you slept
I remember your first spanking
We....both....wept

Watching you grow
Has been my joy
At times I wish

You could stay little forever
Honestly, I don't think
I'll ever be ready
For you to start dating boys

I can't imagine
My life without you
But if for some reason
God decides to call you home
I will live in your memory
And carry you with me
In my heart
So I am never alone

Even though I may think
He called you home too soon
I will never forget
How you started to bloom

My angel, my princess
You will forever be my special girl
Even in your absence
You will be apart of my world

Our bond will never be broken
Our love will transcend time
My baby girl
The words "I love you"
Should never go unspoken

So, my daughter
From my lips to God's ears
Mommy's love will never fade
Even through the years

The Evolution of Me

Born into this world a red-haired little girl
Big brown eyes and deep-dish dimples took over my face
Like with most babies, people oohed and awed

But as I grew older, a transformation took place
Becoming an awkward looking teenage girl
Teasin' and tautin' took over my world

Childhood abuses I kept to myself
Concealed them very well
So, dark secrets I now keep to myself

They dwell in the very heart of me
Takin' over all my dreams and fantasies

As I evolve into womanhood
I struggled to find peace within
I managed to lose my very best friend
Me

But someway, somehow I've got to get her back
Get my life back on track
So I find my souls release
As I put pen to paper
My demons cease

They slowly lose their grip
As I begin to find myself

I now begin to mold myself
Into a person of worth
This is my rebirth

I've found the person I desire to be
As I continue on with the evolution of me

My Sins

Forgive me Father
For I have sinned

I have sinned
Against Man-
Kind, my soul was blind
To the hurt and pain
Playin' deadly games
With words
Not unheard
From vicious lips
I ripped
Hearts apart
From the start
Of friendships
And relationships
Folks weren't equipped
To deal with me
Spreading hurt, but not intentionally
Or could it be
I was just being selfish
Doin' me

Forgive me Father
For I have sinned

I have sinned
With evil thoughts

Plottin' my enemies demise
I devised
My master plan
But my heart can't withstand
Blood being shed
By my hands
So I try to understand
My hate for my fellow man

I drop down
To my knees
As I plead
For mercy
And forgiveness
I confess
To him
All my sins
Prayin' that tomorrow
I won't sin again
But it lives
In the hearts
Of Man-
Kind, sometimes we all go blind
From our sins
Within
Our hearts and minds

So I'll just make it a point
To repent
Again and again
Please forgive me Father
For I have sinned

Buffalo Soldiers

Top-notch soldiers
Since the late eighteen hundreds
Freedom Fighters
Civil Rights Leaders
Men of Honor
Are just a few monikers
They go by

Buffalo Soldiers
A name given by the Cheyenne Indians
A name they accept with pride

Buffalo Soldiers
Fought for freedom and equality
Buffalo Soldiers
Fought for an un-accepting country

Unaccepted as men
In a country they and their ancestors helped to build
A country, built on their backs, blood, sweat and tears
Thoughts of freedom grew in their minds over the years

Selfless acts of bravery
Seen in every Black Infantry
Henry O. Flipper
Charles Young
Pompey Factor
Just to name a few

For your efforts
We thank you

Thank you
For enduring racism
And proving us a worthy race
Thank you
For your magnificence
And securing our place
In history and
In this nation

Thank you
For your tireless acts
And your dedication

Thank you
For your years of service
To this country

Thank you
For paving the way
For others and for me

Great African-American Soldiers
We honor your sacrifice
Your legacy
And all you represent
Guided by His will
Your strength was and is heaven sent

For all you have done
And continue to do
We honor the very essence of you
Buffalo Soldiers!

I Write the Poems

I write the poems
That makes the world think
In the blink of an eye
Words from these pages
Tug on ya heart strings
And make even the hardest thug cry

Words so intense
They spark a fire in ya conscious
Make you contemplate
The meaning of life
Make you see the consequence
Of being a slave to a gun and knife

I write the poems
That make you want to
Put down your weapons
And pick up a book
Have you seein'
That your life
Is worth a second look

You're not bound by street violence
You don't have to suffer in silence
There are so many wonderful things
You can do in your life
Don't continue livin' in strife
Let my words

Lead you to our Savior
'Cause He has the power
To save you, me, him and her

I write the poems
That frees enslaved souls
Boggling ya mind
Makin you lose ya self control
Titillating ya 3rd eye

Provoking sincere thought
And conversation
Delivering instant liberation

I write the poems
That teaches truth
To our misguided youth
Hollow-point words
100% deadly
To ignorance
Check my stance
This ain't a game
These words are for real
Definitely not Jesus
But my words still heal

I write the poems
That brings sensuality
Back to sex
Reviving intercourse
With mere words
Saving marriages
On the brink of divorce
Sexy words
Increase imagination
To the height of ecstasy

Freeing the inhibited
To live out
Their fantasies

Thought provoking
Sensual words
Placed intricately
On pages
Revive desperate nerves
Breathing life
Into him, her, and them
I am the one
That writes those poems!

Nocturnal Poems

At night
Words come to me
In various forms of poetry

Verse after verse
Invades my mind
Takin' me on a journey to a different place and time

I try to rest
But poems bounce around my thoughts
Playin' hide and seek, tryin not to get caught

Nocturnal Poems
Creep through my dreams
Playin' like a movie…..scene after scene

Nightly poems
Run rampant from beginning to end
Only to stop before I reach my pad and pen

Nocturnal Poems
Keep me tossin' and turnin'
Like fuel to a fire, my passion keeps burnin'

Addicted to these words
Addicted to this feelin'
Nocturnal Poems sound so appealin'

Can't shake these verbs
Can't shake these words
Can't shake these metaphors
After one line, I want more....and more

My mind is the stage
For Nocturnal Poems to rehearse
Flows so amazing, I sometimes spit them in reverse

Appealin' so sound Poems Nocturnal
Feelin this to addicted
Words these to addicted

Now form correct to return I
Stop
Reverse
I return to correct form now

At night
My mind drifts to words in an open forum
Sweet haunting continues through these Nocturnal Poems

Monday Blues

My weekend has ended much too soon
Monday morning came
And my heart filled with gloom
Not enough time
To spend with
Family and
Friends
Why did my weekend have to end?

Not enough time in those 2 little days
Not enough time for her and mommy to play
Not enough time to finish all my chores
Okay, so I got to the windows
But damn
I forgot about the floors

Those 2 little days slip away
So fast
My head can't stop spinning
Why doesn't my weekend
Ever seem to last
Long enough
For me to enjoy them
I'm constantly sinkin'
Every time I try to swim

0500 Monday morning
My alarm rings

And I feel restless and confused
The dreadful beginning
Of another long week
And I can never seem to shake
These Monday Blues!

Juneteenth

Emancipate me
From this confederate land
Emancipate me
From my master's hand

Give me rights
Give me freedom
Let me own land
And improve upon my wisdom

Beat us no more
For we are now free
Beat us no more
We are asserting our equality

We are no longer property
We've become people again
My people rejoice
Slavery finally came to an end

Let us remember June 19th, 1865
Let us celebrate this victory
Let us live beyond this day
As we mark this day in our history

Lift every voice in song
Lift every voice in prayer
No longer are we slaves

We are free from the burdens we used to bare

Juneteenth, a new beginning
From Texas to D.C.
We have no more worries
'Cause we are finally free

The Strength of a Woman

My sistas
Some of you have lost your way
Forgot that we helped make it possible
To be here in this day

My sistas
Some of you have forgotten your worth
We are more than just mother-whores
Used to give birth

We are more than our breast sizes
We are more than our asses
Thighs
And hips
We stand along side men
Enduring all relationships

We helped build nations
Birthed kings and soldiers through our wombs
We helped build pyramids and ancestral tombs

We have been Queens
Inventors
Entrepreneurs
And political activist

We find strength to go on
After attacks from perverted rapists

Go on after failed marriages
Losing our jobs
And being hurt by our kids

We have endured hatred
We have endured racism
We have endured sexism
And have still persevered
This nation was also built on our blood, sweat and tears

We need to stop
Selling ourselves short
Dressing ½ naked in videos
Answering to the call of bitches and hoes
Thinking that our worth lies only between our thighs

1 night stands
And booty calls are not all we are good for
Baby girl our worth is immeasurable
And that fact we should never ignore

We built underground railroads
We freed slaves
We fought in wars
We died on the battle fields
And we are what men crave

Our strength knows no boundaries
Our strength has no limits
When they said we couldn't
Damn it, we still did it

We've made millions
Ran companies
Lead troops
And raised families

We play vitals roles in our communities

James Brown said it best
"This is a man's world
But it wouldn't be nothing
Without a woman or a girl"
So remember your worth
That shit is as precious as a pearl

Never forget
What you are capable of
Never lose yourself for any man
And don't ever forget
The strength of a Woman

Strange Fruit

I've heard stories
Of southern strange fruit
Hanging from trees
Swaying softly in the wind

There were no seeds
For this strange fruit
It was not something you planted

This strange fruit
Just appeared nightly
In southern trees
Swaying softly in the wind

This strange fruit
Was not meant to be picked
It wasn't meant to be eaten

This strange fruit
Were the bodies of black men
Who had been beaten
'Til they had no life left

Left for all to see
Left as a warning
That there was still room on that same tree

Strange fruit burnt

Images so painful
So horrible
That families never forgot
And were never mentally free

Strange fruit
Swaying softly in the wind
On unwilling branches
Placed by the hands
Of sinful men

Strange fruit burnt
Images so painful
So Horrible
That families never forgot
And were never mentally free

Strange
Southern
Fruit
Swaying softly in the wind
Strange
Southern
Fruit
Hung from branches of unwilling trees
Strange
Southern
Fruit
A painful part of our history
Strange
Southern
Fruit
We are finally free

Unspoken Melodies

Without words being spoken
Your eyes tell me an elaborate story
Of love making sessions
You'd love for us to share

The longer I gaze into your eyes
The faster my heart begins to beat
The anticipation of your touch
Makes my soul quiver

Your eyes are so captivating
They show me your soul
And allow me to see your true beauty
Deep
Beautiful
Brown
Eyes
Oh how they entice me

Your lips silent
No words need to be spoken
They invite me in closer
Close enough to taste your nectar
Sweet
Succulent
Lips
Tease my very soul with each kiss

My body begins to play
An unspoken melody of movements
Moving
Slowly
So you can conduct your orchestra……..
Me

Make me play for you
A tune that resonates to your core
Sweet
Simple
Sounds
Of pure pleasure

My melody is yours
My soul is yours
My body is yours

Make me play your tune
Tonight
Tomorrow
After breakfast
Before dinner
I'll play it only for you

No words need to be spoken
As we gaze into each others eyes
Our melody plays loudly
Through our souls

The stars become jealous
Of our illuminating love
The constellations become jealous
As we are more beautiful than they
Symphonies envy our tune
As we strike chords more beautifully

Thunder applauds the bass in our tune
You are my sun
And I am your moon
Silently we enjoy each others tune

Unspoken Melodies

The First Father's Day

I see your face beaming with pride
Unconditional love and joy well up inside
The ultimate protector you've become
Flesh of your flesh, you and I are one

We bond at feedings, diaper changes and story time
So no matter how many seeds you breed
Each one is just as special, so you feed
Our souls and minds
With all your knowledge and wisdom
Your life of teaching has only just begun

Each of our births
Marked a new first Father's Day for you
You treat us all like a dream come true

As we get older
Sometimes we put undue stress on you
But no matter what
We know we can always count on you

We may not know it now
But one day we will grow to appreciate all you tried to do
All the lessons you taught
All the spankings we received for doing wrong
We will learn you were only trying to make us strong

Real life is hard and certainly not fair

But you walked us through it all to show how much you care
Some lessons we had to ultimately learn on our own
But you've always lent your ear and advice even though we think
    we are too grown

Thank you for fathering your seeds
And showing how a good father should be
Thank you for fatherly love
Thank you for fatherly advice
Thank you for being there during my darkest nights

Auntie
Ode to Olivia A. Fletcher

You've become our rock
Saving no time for yourself
You continue to go, non-stop
Taking care of the family
Hopefully you know
How special you are to me

You have been there
While others play the back
You are the force
That is keeping our family on track

I am so thankful
To have you in my life
We've shared long talks
And you've helped ease my strife

My trouble, my pain
Always putting others first
And never concerned with worldly gains

God has put aside
A special room in Heaven
Just for you
Packed with all your favorite things
A place for you to rest
When this life is through

You've lent your ears
Dried our tears
Dished out tough love
When it was needed
Given me advice
Your words, I took to heart
And I always heeded them

Sink or swim
I knew I could always
Count on you
Cherishing the person you are
I wish only happiness for you

Auntie
More than just a relative
You are the backbone
Of this family

I say prayers for you
So at night
You can rest easily

Thank you
For doing what I can't
In my absence

Thank you
For being there
For my mother and your mother too
I am forever grateful
And this is my Ode to You,
Auntie

The Secret of my Depression

Sometimes my mind tells me
That I shouldn't be happy with me
Sometimes my mind says
That society deems me not pretty enough
Not skinny enough
That I don't have enough junk in my trunk
That my hair is not long enough
That my breasts need to be bigger
That my stomach needs to be flatter

My mind tells me that I need to starve myself
Instead...........I eat more
My mind tells me that I need to work out twice a day
Instead...........I just sit around and eat more
My mind is tellin me that I am not pretty enough for anyone
So, I eat and I eat

I eat 'cause food is my only friend
I eat 'cause only food understands me
I eat when I'm happy
I eat when I'm sad

Food comforts me
But it destroys my self-esteem
The very thing I try to avoid
Calls to me
It beckons me
Like crack

It helps destroy me

The secret of my depression
Is my obsession to be perfect
But perfection in my eyes
Has been distorted
And my true perception of me
Has been aborted
From my mind

My third eye is now blind
To how beautiful I really am
But this obsession I can't shake
See, I've come to realize
As time passes by
That the real secret of my depression
Is my own regression in my thoughts
Not remembering that my beauty still remains
Despite the few pounds I've gained

I am still beautiful
And as my mind throws off its chains
I will remain
The beautiful person I've always been
In my own skin
As I let go of my obsession
My mind ceases to be the secret of my depression

100 Reasons
Ode to Myrtle Brents

Today we celebrate you
100 years you've made it through
Seen things we could never fathom
Seen our people killed at random
You've made it through the great wars
And The Depression
You manage to rise above
All of life's oppressions

100 plus reasons
We have to adore you
For giving us strength
To make it through
Our own hard times and everyday life
You made it possible for us to be better
Sisters
Brothers
Cousins
Husbands and
Wives

You've shown us
What it means to survive
You never lost your focus
You always continued to strive
For the best
No matter what obstacles were in your way

You took care of your family
Every…..single….day

Generation after generation
You still continue to share
Your love and wisdom
Through you
His will has been done

He has blessed us
With your presence
For 100 years
He has kept you going
And allowed us to revere
You

For all you have accomplished
And all you continue to do
We marvel at His masterpiece
You!

Season after season
We've had 100 plus reasons
To love you
Granny

Haters

Due to the blessings
The Almighty has bestowed
Upon me
I've encountered numerous
Haters.........Hating on me

You see
I know I've made mistakes
Taken some wrong turns in life
But at the same time
Those mistakes
Have made me the woman
I am today

I may not be proud
Of my every decision
Some have caused
Repercussions
Pain and humiliation
In my life and in others'

But I'm human
And I have to make mistakes
In order to grow

But haters.....
They broadcast my mistakes
As if they were perfect

Not knowing
I've been down on my knees
And He has heard me repent

Haters let their jealousy
Consume them
And since misery loves company
They use their words

To attempt to bring me down
Right along with them

But I've got my life vest on
So this time
I won't sink
While I swim
Stroking through
This sea of hate
I put my trust in Him
So He owns my fate

So keep hating on me
Keep sprinkling dirt on my name
Your actions
Only bring me more fame
Your words spark an interest
In what Soul Food Poems
Is really about
So keep my name in ya mouth
And keep building my clout

Keep that hate alive
Coursing through your veins
Remember its S O U L F O O D P O E M S
That's how you spell my name
Keep hating on me

Day and night
Say what you will
Just remember to spell my name right

Put your hand in the air
If you can relate
Not too long ago
You were the ones
Haters decided to berate

But let them be
So they can continue
To do their jobs
They need a purpose
So they don't feel
Completely worthless

For me
I know who I am
And where I'm going
He runs my life
So I'm constantly growing
Keep hating on me
If that's what you choose
He's at the helm of my life
SO I WILL NOT LOSE!

Slow Jams Pt. 2

One day on A Long Walk
Me and Those Dreamin' Eyes of Mine
Spotted a gorgeous man
Who had the most Pretty Brown Eyes
As we began to talk
I told him I was All Cried Out over love

We sat down on a park bench
And he told me to Slide Over
He whispered softly in my ear
Baby Come to Me
He said Yesterday is gone
So it's time I started to embrace
These Happy Feelings

He said there were so many Reasons not to give up on love
Then he took my hand and said,
Come On and Go With Me
Over The Rainbow
So we can find a Religious Love

At first I was scared
So I told him
And I am Telling You, I'm Not Going
He looked deep into my eyes
Then he said, I Can't Go On Without You
So don't worry because I'll be with you
Until The End of Time

Over the years we've grown closer
So we Can't Stay Away from one another
Both of us have the sweetest Love Hangover

With a smile on my face
I told him baby, You Bring Me Joy
I Can't Tell You Why we still share Secret Rendezvous, I said
And his response was because baby U Got It Bad!
All I know is that I'm So Gone
Over our Sweet Love

One day he had to leave to tend to some business
So he left me a love letter
It read;

My Dear I'm Leaving On a Midnight Train to Georgia
And I just wanted to let you know that I've Fallen deeply in love
with you. Honestly, I think I'D Die Without You. I know I'll
always Love, Need and Want You Baby. Please Tell Me If You
Still Care.

So I decided to write him back
And I said;

If You Don't Know Me By Now, then I guess you will figure
it out in the Next Lifetime. Didn't Cha Know that I'm All In
Love With You? I Miss You and my love for you is not Just My
Imagination (Running Away With Me). I'm Overjoyed to have
you in my life, and while you are gone you can be my Computer
Love. When you come home, I'm Gonna Love You Just A Little
More, Baby, while we make love in the Purple Rain. So until
then,

Good-Bye Love

Follow Me

Follow me on this journey where rhyme has no reason
Where everyday it's the same old season
Walk down the street that leads to nowhere
Where the rich refuse to care
About the poor who suffer through their daily dose of
degradation

Where escaping the ghetto is the greatest emancipation
Follow me past the crack addict who swears this will be her last
hit
Where the prostitute swears this will be her last trick
Follow me past the school with no books
Where young girls are obsessed with attaining the perfect look

Follow me down the corridor that leads to nevermore
Follow me past the war that has no meaning
Past the hungry child that can't hide his screaming
Follow me past the street where pain runs too deep
Where teens have no choice but to live out their destiny
From corner to corner and street to street

Follow me through the ghetto where most dreams cease to
grow
Where hope is a 4 letter word that seldom heard
Where adulthood is stunted by bullets and jail
Where no one cares if they make it to heaven or hell
Follow me into a reality that could corrode the skin with lethal
doses of deadly sin

Where encouraging words fall upon deaf ears
And abandoned children live everyday in fear

Follow me across the state where deception has become the
reality
Where saying I love you has become just a formality
Follow me on the journey through space and time
To find a place where you can free your trapped mind
Follow me through a dream that desperately wants to become
more than just a figment of your imagination
Where your soul can find its desired salvation

Follow me through the 60's south where hatred ceased to exist
Where blacks and whites were able to coexist
Follow me in reverse as we descend from the slave ships and
keep Africa alive
Where its land became rich and the whole country survived

Follow me through the perverse criminal mind back to a time
where they were still pure
Where they took a different path in life that allowed them to
endure….everyday dilemmas without resorting to violence
and having everyone suffer that consequence
Follow me to a time when Pastors have a captive audience
Where everyone illuminated with their benevolence
Follow me on this journey, follow me on this trip, follow me
through this place and contemplate what was seen here and
how things could actually be
Rebuke the dark side of society and cherish all the good
Eliminate the ghettos and create prosperous neighborhoods
It's time to make this into a reality
Now take my hand and follow me

I have a Dream

I have a dream
That Martin Luther King's
Vision
Was a reality
Not just a borderline fallacy
Disguised mostly by meaningless gestures
From those who would like to keep us sequestered

I have a dream
That his life
Wasn't prematurely brought to an end
That he wasn't
Taken down by the sin
That lived in the hearts of men

I have a dream
That Martin Luther King
Was able to put an end to hatred and racism
Which lives within the human race
So we could all embrace
One another
Like sisters and brothers
No matter your color

To see his ideals
Grow without hesitation
Ending all forms of discrimination
That would emit the ultimate exhilaration

Throughout our nation

He was the epitome of a leader
Putting the needs of his race
Above his own
He believed in turning the other cheek
So for others sins, he atoned

A gift from heaven
He suffered through hell
An ambassador for justice

He penned the "Letter from Birmingham Jail"
Describing the injustices taking place in our country.......
Within the black community
His efforts paved the way
Allowing us to see better days

He led marches
And boycotts
Helped found the Southern Christian Leadership Conference
He was a husband
A father
Pastor and
Friend
He was so many things
To so many people
Even after his life came to an end

Community Activist
Civil Rights Leader
Author
Nobel Peace Prize Winner
And a quintessential human being
Thanks to Martin Luther King
We are living part of his dream

The Other Me

5 feet 5 ½ inches I stand
Frame slightly larger than what I desire
But I still see the beauty in me

I am Me, but not the Me he desires
Not the frame that sets his soul on fire
Not the red boned
Thick thighed
Firmed assed
Big breasted
Woman that lives within his fantasy

I am the reality that he can physically see
I am Me, but not the other Me he'd like me to be
I am the Me that has grown tired of not being able to be his
    fantasy

He can't see the love I have for him
He can't understand how my soul adores him
He blindly looks at me searchin' for his fantasy

Body untouched by the hands of plastic surgeons
I refuse to abuse the beauty that is Me
I refuse to let mental scars bind me
I refuse to let someone else's fantasy become my reality

I am Me, but not the other Me that he lusts for
Endlessly

I can't be anything other than this beauty
That has already graced me
I may not be perfect to some
Nevertheless, I am still fabulous
And that's what I believe

I aim to please
Me
Because my beauty is obvious to me

Made from His image
I dare not change what He has created
Thanks to Him, my beauty glows and will never be underrated

I will not be turned into a silicone princess
Changin for anyone but myself
Now, that would be so senseless
I may never be the other Me that rules his fantasies
But damn it, I am always going to be the sexiest Me

A Mind Freed

My mind was once closed on life
I never imagined I would grow out of this thought
Instead of finding a way to deal with my scars
I suppressed all the negativity in my life
I suppressed all the pain
All the mean things people said or did to me
I suppressed the evils that exploited my childhood innocence

I buried it so deep it began to eat at my soul
Corrode my heart
Erase my dreams
Pump lies through my veins
I could no longer give or receive love
And it began to hurt

My soul felt empty
I couldn't comprehend why my life felt so meaningless
Why love was evading me
Why I thought so negatively
This pain was growin
To the point that I would cry myself to sleep

My 22nd birthday hit
And I still couldn't understand
This path that my life was takin

Then one day while I sat alone in my dorm room
My thoughts began to swirl

As I sat Bible in hand
My eyes began to fill with tears
My actions became so clear

All the trauma from my childhood
Came to light
By now, tears were streamin' down my face
My life began to make sense

As I read my Bible, my skin began to tingle
His words were speakin' to me
His words were settin' me free
His words opened up my closed mind

I began to feel liberated
No longer was my soul sedated
My emotions were no longer numb
My life had finally begun

My third eye could finally see
No longer was I going to live in misery
I could see all my life's possibilities
Since my mind had finally been freed

The Sins of the Father

Let he who is without sin
Cast the first stone
Sins being made by mankind daily
Yet we never atone

We sin with our minds
We sin with our lips
We sin with our hands
We sin with our eyes
Damning our souls
And creating our own demise

The sins of the father
Come back to haunt mankind
Yet we accept no responsibility
Acting as if we were blind
We've developed tunnel vision
Refusing to see life's incisions
Placed on our souls
By making bad decisions

We shun Asians
Thanks to Cho Seung-Hui
We shun Arabs
Thanks to 9/11
Thinking that our souls
Are so perfect
That we will definitely

Wind up in heaven

Children growing up without real parental guidance
But we blame them
For turning into a nuisance
Most of mankind lives in the 7 deadly sins
Lust
Gluttony
Greed
Sloth
Wrath
Envy and
Pride
We lie to ourselves
Not realizing
That we are messed up inside

Our sins are planted like seeds
Infecting the children we breed
Hate is fertilizing young minds
As they become inclined
To perpetuate violence
No longer living in silence

Snap
Their minds break
Innocent lives they take
As the seed of hate
Has blossomed in their soul
They've lost all control

Too late to get their lives back
On the right track
Tracks on her arms and thighs
Living everyday just to get high
Introduced to the drug game

By her father's street fame
He disowned her and feels no shame

The sins of her father
Came back to haunt her
Yet he accepts no responsibility
Acting as if he was blind
He's developed tunnel vision
Refusing to see life's incisions
He's placed on her soul
From his bad decisions

Innocence dripping out of open incisions
Young minds confused
'Cause their life is not how they envisioned
So easy to do wrong
They refuse to do right
As they set their sights
On being the next big thing

They contemplate their legacy
Somehow, you will remember me
Somehow, I'm going down in history
So make no mistake
Or it'll be your life I take

I'm going to sell the most drugs
I'm going to do the biggest school shooting
I'm going to start the biggest riot
And do the most looting

The hate seed has flourished
And continues to grow
Turn a blind eye if you like
But remember, you reap what you sew

The sins of the father
Come back to haunt mankind
Yet we accept no responsibility
Acting as if we were blind
We've developed tunnel vision
Refusing to see life's incisions
Placed on our souls
By making bad decisions

Sensual

Sensual is stolen moments
We share during the day
That quick five or ten minute getaway
We sit and gaze into each other's eyes
In the absence of words
Our body language speaks loudly

Sensual is soft kisses
Gently placed all over our bodies
From enduring forehead kisses
To the napes of our necks
And playful kisses on our thighs

Sensual is cuddling during the night
Being nestled within the warmth
Of each others bodies
Feeling secure in each others arms

Sensual is mental love making
Seductive phone calls throughout the day
Building anticipation of what is to come
Allowing our imaginations to run free
With thoughts of passion

Sensual is your natural scent
Drawing me in closer
Begging me to engulf myself in you

Sensual is alluring massages
Releasing unwanted tension
Allowing passion to take over
Replacing stress with love

Sensual is showers and baths together
Washing away each others insecurities
And replacing them with trust
Towel drying one another
Letting nature and our natural beauty take its course

Sensual is finding ways to keep those fires burning
After years of being together
Creating new fantasies to live out
And starting each day anew

Sensual is.........

Simply Beautiful

Simply beautiful
Is the love we share
Not a simple love
But, complex
Complex in a way
That keeps our love
Refreshing

Refreshing
Is each moment we share
Lost in time
Forgetting our worries
And appreciating
The beauty of us

Simply
Intoxicating
Is your love
I inebriate myself
With thoughts of you
Like forbidden fruit
I lust for you
Passionately

Passionately
I crave your touch
My fantasies provide
Vivid imagery

Allowing me to taste you
Even in my dreams

Simply beautiful
Is the life we share
Living each day
Without fear
Because you've got my back
And I've got yours

Simply beautiful
Is the ability to accept physical changes
And still love our inner beauty
To embrace change
And still find each other
Sexy

Sexy
Is your lips
Your eyes
Your arms
Your smile
Your soul

Simply beautiful
Is you and I
Mentally intertwined
For eternity

Simply beautiful

Black History

Black History takes me back to Africa
To a prosperous land that once possessed great beauty
To a land that once thrived with us as Kings and Queens

Black History takes me back to the first time we were sold
To us being taken from our native land
To a fear of not knowing what was ahead of us

Black History takes me back to the beginning of slavery
To chains and whips
To families being separated and missing each other

Black History takes me back to our innate desire to be free
To the Underground Railroad
To learning how to read despite the threat of death

Black History to me is
Freedom Marches
Bus Boycotts
City-wide riots
Police Dogs and
Being Hosed

Black History to me is
Surviving all odds
Standing up to racism and
Organizing Sit-Ins

Harriet
Sojourner
Frederick
Medgar
Martin
Malcolm
The Panther Party
And all those who paved our way

For your struggle
We have no other words to say
But Thank You

You instilled in us
Hope
Pride
And knowledge on how to survive

We honor your life long accomplishments
We thank you today and everyday
Thanks to you, our rights are apparent

Black History is our right to an education
Our right to equal housing
Our right to equal employment
Our right to civil equality
Our right to vote

Black History is so much more than 28 days on a calendar
Black History is so much more than just a struggle
Black History is our past, present and future
Black History is our never ending story
And this is what Black History means to me

Fighting for Attention

Silent cries go unanswered everyday
Souls try to reach out
They plead for attention
Beg for understanding
Lust for affection

Just a simple hug
A meaningful kiss
A shoulder to cry on
Someone to just....
Listen

Listen
With more than your ears
Listen
With your eyes
Listen
With your heart
Just listen

Listen
Listen to those souls
As you pass them by
They are begging you to hear their story
They are begging
Begging for you not to judge them
Rather understand their struggle
Their suffering

Their pain

Listen
Listen as their hearts cry out to you
Cry out for mercy
They need you to be a friend
To treat them as human
Not as a burden on you or society
They need you to just
Listen

Listen
Listen as your soul begins to relate
There is a part of you
That
Understands
That has traveled down a dark road
Leading
Nowhere
But
To hurt and pain

Yet you managed to recover
To find yourself again
To get your life back on track
Because....someone....just
Listened

Listen
Listen with more than your ears
Listen
With your eyes
Listen
With your heart
Because someone is silently
SILENTLY

Fighting for
Your
Attention

Lost, Generation X

Generation X
That's the generation
Who sees hard work as a chore
Instead, they'd rather be hard core
Sagging jeans
And oversized Tee's
Is their uniform of choice
Street cred is their only goal
And you'd better make sure
They know you're a friend
Not a foe

Generation X
That's the generation
Who's proud to call black women
Bitches and Hoes
Even young boys see fit to degrade our women
But get pissed when someone like Don Imus does the same
    thing
Now ain't that a trip, like hearing it from a black mans lips
Doesn't also sting

Generation X
That's the generation
That takes no part in today's politics
So they'd rather sit
And watch their streets
Go from bad

To worse
Not even scared straight
From seeing their homies
Laid out in that hearse

Generation X
That's the generation
That will rob, steal and kill
To get what's yours
Too scared to make it on their own
So taking yours
Is all they've come to know
For PS3's, Ipods, new kicks
And more
They'll come, guns drawn
Kicking in your front door
Better pray you're not home
When they come to do their deed
Otherwise down on your knees
You'll have to plead
But your fate is already determined
Since they're fueled by greed
They'll proceed
On with your death
'Til there's nothing left
Of the things you worked hard to earn
Your possessions have now become their bragging rights

Generation X
That's the generation
That vows to become the biggest drug lord
The next hottest rapper
The next biggest pimp
Fame
That's the only thing they're after
They want the bling

The numerous cars
The house featured on Cribs
Their only concern,
Becoming the next ghetto superstar

Fuck school
And an education
Their rise to fame
That's all they're contemplating
Lost
Lost to understanding
What it took to get us here
Lost to the knowledge
Of knowing our true struggles
Of moving past
Our most horrible years

When will they open their eyes
When will they finally get involved
Generation X
Slipping more and more
Away from our struggles
Slipping
More and more
Away from being an asset to themselves
And our community
Slipping
More and more
Towards that thug mentality
While we pay the cost
Generation X
-AKA-
Generation Lost

Broken
Ode to Mistreated Animals

Hunted
I have now become the prey
I used to roam free
Free in my native land
Surviving
Surviving the way my instincts taught me
Living
Living the way nature intended

Stalked
I have become sought after
To provide amusement
For those who are only amused
By their wicked sense of humor
Picking me and my family off
For sheer....delight

Stolen
Stolen from my birth place
Transported to foreign lands
Beaten and abused
Stripped of my soul
My will
My pride
Stripped of the fight in me

Taunted

Taunted by humans
By bars
By whips
Made to live in conditions
That are....beneath me
Bringing my seeds
Into a cruel society

A society
That shows me no respect

That invades my domain
And ridicules me
When I defend my domain
As if "Society"
Doesn't do the same
But when I do it
It's a problem
A crime
And a shame
So "Society" hunts me down
Telling me
I'm to blame
Minutes before they sentence me to death

They sentence me to death
Every time I do
What nature intended me to
Every time I get fed up
And fight back
Every time I get fed up
And remind them
How powerful I truly am
Every time I get fed up
And put an end
To their inhumane treatment

Of me
And my family

Yet
They show no signs
Of slowing down
Of not constantly hunting me
Stalking me
Stealing me
Raping me
Of my pride

So they continue
Degrading me
Whipping me
Starving me
Forcing me....to do tricks
Forcing me....to wear clothes

Forcing me....to live in fake surroundings
Forcing me....to entertain humans
Leaving me
Ultimately
Broken

Rise

Society has drifted
Drifted into an abyss
An abyss of hopelessness
Only we refuse to see
See exactly how far back
We have drifted

The black community
Has digressed
Into a state of mental slavery
We have trapped our minds
Enslaved our own thoughts
Imprisoned our youth
Degraded ourselves

We have become
Our own modern day blackface
Humiliating ourselves
In videos
And on the news
We have become
Our own worst enemy
Killing more of our own
Than the KKK ever did
Stealing from our own
Raping our own
Selling drugs to our own

We as a race
Have given up
We have given up
On being responsible
For our own
We have given up
On raising our youth
As a community
We have given up
On educating our youth
We have given up
On doing for ourselves

And not depending on welfare
We have given up
On ensuring our young girls
Aren't just having babies
For the sake of having babies

Now
Now is the time for us
To rise up
We need to rise up
And provide a better school system
For our youth
We need to rise up
And rebuild our own communities
We need to rise up
And instill pride in our youth
We need to rise up
And ensure we have a voice
In our nation
We need to rise up
And utilize our right to vote
We need to rise up
And teach our youth

About our past
About the struggle
Our ancestors overcame
About our history
From Africa to America

We need to rise up
And take a stand
Against racism that still exists
We need to rise up
Rise up
Rise up
Rise up
Rise
As a people
Rise
As a community
Rise
Within our nation
Rise
Rise to the occasion

Rise
Rise now
And keep rising
Don't ever look back
Just
Rise!

The First Black President

Change
Change is the tone
In this 2008 election
Change
Change is the focus
Of all the candidates

Our nation must change
It must change to survive
It must change to keep hope alive
It must change to progress
It must change to thrive

It must change
Taxes
Health Care
The economy
It must change
How the rich get richer
And the poor stay poor

It must change
Welfare
The prison system
The ghettos
And job opportunities

It must change

And bring the troops home
Make a firm decision about our borders
And report REAL news

Change
That is what Barack Obama
Is calling for
Change
That is his agenda
The first black president
This is what America
Is ready for

The first black president
Will give hope
Hope to the black community
He is showing us
That we can make a difference
He is showing us
That we are capable
He is showing us
That we are worthy
To hold our country's highest position

The first black president
Will inspire our nation
To get along
The first black president
Will inspire our nation
To unite
The first black president
Will inspire our youth
To dream big
And see that their dreams
Come true

The first black president
Will truly go down in history
He will claim his place
He will spark a flame in us
That will finally wake us up
He will be
Our much needed epiphany

The first black president
Will bring about
What we need most
Change

Her Story

Don't judge her
Until you have walked a mile in her shoes
You don't know......
Her story

Her story
May be hard for you to understand
She didn't grow up
Unscathed by life
She traveled down roads
Some people only see...
In nightmares
Yet
She is still here

Her story
Has others thankful
They didn't endure
These hardships
She did what she had to
In order to survive
And yes
She....is....still....here

Her story
Is complex
Just listen
As I break it down

She grew up in the streets
The corner was her savior
No food to eat
Begging folks to save her
Society turned a blind eye
Passing her by
While watchin' her…..
Cry

She slipped
Down a slope

Of no hope
Dreams crushed
By wicked souls
Putting her goals
In chokeholds

Forcing her
To degrade herself
For their wealth
Passing on mere dollars
Her soul hollers
For peace
At least
A chance
Not just a glance
At a good life

She sees
A ray of hope
At the end of that slope
'Cause she's focused now
Knowing with faith
She'll make it somehow

She leaves behind
Her tattered past
Finding peace at last

She's resilient
The fight in her is still alive
She always knew
She had the strength
To survive
She just needed
The opportunity to arise
Before her eyes
So she could grab on tight
Climbing out of the pit
Of hopelessness

She is
The mother hustling
To feed her kids
She is
The prostitute struggling

To get off the corner
She is
The homeless girl
Still getting her education
She is
All the women
That have had to overcome obstacles
She is
A survivor
And this is
Her story

News Worthy

Remember when the news
Was worth watching
Remember when reporters
Actually cared about
What they reported on
Remember when the news
Made you feel informed

Today
The news contains
The latest Britney Spears fiasco
Or what Paris Hilton is doing
Today
The new is all about
Who got caught sleeping with whom
And what celebrity just got arrested
Today
The news talks about
The outcome of the "Flavor of Love"
Or who "New York" chose as her mate

I need my news
To inform me about
The tragedies in Sierra Leone
Or the children
Still starving around the world
I need my news
To keep me updated

On the soldiers in Iraq
Or the situation concerning our borders

Tell me more about
The housing situation
Tell me more about
The new tax laws affecting the middle class
Enlighten me more
On the rebuilding of New Orleans
Entice my thoughts
With the good going on
Around the world

Bring me to tears
Talking about senseless tragedies

Stop insulting us
With watered down
Meaningless news
We are sick of
Listening to celebrities' business
We are bored to tears
Hearing worthless stories about
Britney Spears
Lindsay Lohan
Paris Hilton
Michael Jackson
Anna Nicole Smith
Eddie Murphy
And everyone else
That has nothing to do with
How our society is shaping up
Or healthcare reform
Or homelessness in America
And our failing school system

Inform us about
Things that truly matter
Missing girls and children
Both black and white
Inner-city crime
And domestic violence
Inform us about
Things that are truly...news...worthy!

100% Woman

I came into this world
An innocent little girl
Not viewing others
As anything other
Than human

But as I grew older
Labels were automatically
Placed on me
Trying to define me
Trying to categorize me
As anything other
Than just a woman

Am I a black woman
An African American woman
Or a woman who is
Black.........rather
African American

You see
I am a fourth
Native American
A fourth
Caucasian American
And that makes up
My mother's half of me

I am a fourth
Creole
A fourth
French
And that makes up
My father's half of me

But I am also
100% woman
Despite the swirl
Of colors coursing
Through my veins

I remain
100% Woman

From the curve
Of my bosom
To the canal
Of my womb
Where I birth wisdom
I am 100%
Woman

The label I bare
Reads 100%
Unmistakable
Woman
Handle with care

My exterior is strong
But at times
My soul gets
Weary
So I need to be
Cared for in the

Gentle cycle
As I recycle
My strength

All I ask
Is that you not
Label me
Categorize me
Or catalog me
Just remember
When you look at me
That I am not a black woman
An African American woman
Rather look at me
As a 100% Woman
Undeniably

Educate your Mind

Ladies
It's time we educate our minds
On a new level
To start thinking like most men
That we allow ourselves
To give in
To

See if we flip the script
We can finally get a grip
On how we allow ourselves to be treated
Instead of being abused
We could be
Needed

Open your thoughts to think like them
And it might just scare you
Enough for you to no longer
Give in
To that insincere brotha'
Regardless of color
You know the type
That you allow to sell you his hype
The one who swears
He will never love another like you
But at the club
He's chillin' with his main Boo

Meanwhile you're at home
Cooking a hot meal and keeping the house clean
He's keeping you dazed and confused
Why?
'Cause you've allowed him to

You gave it up on the first night
Playing right into his game
You just knew this was love at first sight
But it took him months to even remember ya name
So he called you things like Shawty and Boo

And you thought it was cute
Not realizing you were just one of a few
That he was juggling at the time
Time moved on and you let him hit again and again
You swore you all had something
You swore that he was more than just a friend

But you forgot to flip the script
To think like him
Why settle down with you
When you accept his disrespect
And continue to let him neglect
You
Why be faithful when you've
Already allowed him to cheat and come back home
Every chance he gets
He will definitely roam

Why?
'Cause you've already shown him
He can do what he wants without remorse
Or regards to your feelings
To him that's so appealing

In his mind
Your conversation goes something like this
Hey Boo slow down
You're moving way too fast
Now just be easy
And come give ya man a kiss
All I want is a quick piece of ass
I'm not looking for something from you that will last
See you're not the type that I consider wifey material
Especially since I can tell you're way too superficial
Besides, I know I'm not the only one you let hit on the first
    night
So really, do expect me to make you my wife?

You forgot to flip the script
And think like him
So you allowed yourself to get caught up
Caught up on good looks
Money and fancy cars
Those were your temptations
Not realizing
You should be looking for someone who could build on a foundation
With liberating conversation
And a supreme mentality

Instead you sacrificed your soul
For an illusion of reality
'Cause you were enticed by his sexuality
He sensed that in you
Used it against you
And you allowed him to venture
In your most precious treasure
Giving him pleasure
At your expense
While you suffer the consequence
Of not educating your mind to think like men

So they can no longer take advantage of women

Learn that what we posses is priceless
And should be treated like a gift
Only to be shared with the worthy
Not with just anyone who looks thirsty
Thirsty in a sense that all they want
Is to strip you of your control and most precious treasure
Just so they can have
Instant
Pleasure

Be smart enough to see through that disguise
Or you'll fall victim to your own demise
Knowledge yourself
Wise your dome
Understand that now is the time
For you to educate your mind

Forever

Can I tell you my deepest secret
Can I share with you
How I feel about you
And have you accept that
Without getting scared off
Or taking advantage of my feelings

See, I just want to love you
Forever
And I'm talking about the kind of love
That allows us to fulfill
Each other's fantasies
The kind of love
Where we can engulf ourselves in
One another
The kind of love
Where our natural scents
Are each other's favorite smell
The kind of love
Where we feel safe in each other's arms
The kind of love
Where we know we would never do each other harm
The kind of love
That allows us to become intertwined
In each other's minds

I just want to love you
Forever

I'm talking about the kind of love
That has us completing each other's sentences
The kind of love
Where I'm your chick on the side, wife, lover and mistress
The kind of love
Where you can't imagine your life without me
The kind of love
That belongs to only us 'cause you've got the lock and I've got the key
The kind of love
That goes beyond the physical attraction
The kind of love
That guarantees complete satisfaction
The kind of love
We've been searching for, for a lifetime
The kind of love
Where I am unmistakably yours and you are unmistakably mine

See,
I'm talking about the kind of love
Where we can grow old together
The kind of love
That other people wish they had
The kind of love
That makes miserable couples
Mad
'Cause they can't figure out
How we got and stayed at this point
In our relationship
I'm talking about the kind of love
That lets us
Read each other's minds
The kind of love
That transcends time

I just want to love you
Forever

Or more like a quarter past infinity
Or an hour past indefinitely
Or a century past a light year
Or until death do us
Part of me can't wait to love you forever
The other part
Wants to love you
Whenever
Wherever
However, I want you to know
I plan on loving you from your hair follicles
To your toes
And
Everywhere in between
The 2 of us I feel so much
Love is all I want to give you
Forever

I'm talking about the kind of love
That lasts until Juvember 98th
The kind of love
That has me making up crazy ass dates
The kind of love
That's not complete if we're not together
Forever
Is how long I want to love you
Until my memory fades
And I can no longer remember
You
Become a feeling that's etched in my thoughts

See,
I'm talking about the kind of love
That makes me smile when I think about you
The kind of love
That has me calling you 10 times a day

The kind of love
Where we sit on the phone and have nothing to say
The kind of love
That makes us both feel like soul mates
The kind of love
Where we constantly feel like we're still on our first date
The kind of love
Where I'm your favorite 3 course meal
The kind of love
Where wanted is how you always feel

I just want to love you
Forever
The kind of love
That when I lay on you
Our hearts beat as 1
The kind of love
That even when I'm angry with you
I fantasize
About
Touching you
Holding you
Kissing you
Needing you
Pleasing
You and I are meant to be together
Forever, or until the end of time

Maybe
Wait
Isn't that the same thing
Forever
And the end of time
Yeah, that does have a nice ring
Our love continues
Coming around full circle, it never ends

Each morning when we arise it constantly begins again

Everyday we are like newly weds
Caught up in the bliss of our love
It just goes on
Forever
Forever, ever
Forever, ever

Perfect Combination

Liberating conversations
We've shared
You've managed to take me there
There
The place I've been searching for
Longing for
You've opened that door

Now
I find myself examining this situation
Because I believe
We are the perfect combination
The student and the teacher
The congregation and the preacher
The sun and the moon
The musical notes and the tune

I've been searching
For some understanding in my life
A way to heal my strife
You've become my light
Leading me out of the dark
What a beautiful start

You've verbally enlightened me
Physically enticed me
Invited me to explore
Me

You awakened my 3rd eye
While you supplied
Knowledge
Like a freshman in college
I listened
I examined
I learned
Then you gave me a turn
To shine
With my mind
Developing my wisdom
So I may become
Whole

Now
I find myself examining this situation
Because I believe
We are the perfect combination
The student and the teacher
The congregation and the preacher
The sun and the moon
The musical notes and the tune

I look forward to each new conversation
As we build on this foundation
You release my frustration
And become my salvation

This is not just fascination
With your mind
But more like admiration
For the person you are
Completing this circle
Of the sun, moon and stars

I enjoy this collaboration
Between you and I
The minutes between our conversations
Builds anticipation
For our next cipher session
Of expression
You've made it a point
To answer all my questions
And not leave me guessin'
We've shared our pasts
And you chose not to judge my indiscretions

Fate crossed our paths
As your ears were tuned in
To the knowledge dripping from my lips
A sudden eclipse
Took over the room
Sparking forgotten wisdom
I had become
Numb
To past teachings
Reason being
My Enlightenment bailed

So I closed my mind
Like the bars of a jail
Cell
Mate you've become
The chosen 1
To unleash in me
The Supreme power of 3
Knowledge, Wisdom and Understanding

Now
I find myself examining this situation
Because I believe

We are the perfect combination
The student and the teacher
The congregation and the preacher
The sun and the moon
The musical notes and the tune

Black History pt.2

Black History
Started as a week
Back in 1926
By Carter G. Woodson

In 1976,
50 years later
Black History Month
Was established

Celebrating African Americans
Celebrating their numerous contributions
Celebrating their sacrifices
And the lives lost
Freeing slaves

Black History
Pays tribute to all Americans
Helping to put an end
To slavery

Black History
Includes presidents
Congressmen
Senators
Policemen
All doing their part
To see our country succeed

With unity
Equality and
Justice

Black History
Celebrates life
Love and
Accomplishments
From communities
Once forgotten
But now thriving
Off memories

Of our ancestors
Surviving

Black History
Tells stories
Of survival
And will
Black History
Tells stories
Of teamwork
And brotherly love

Black History
And American History
Are one in the same
A celebration of
Coming together
Despite our differences

Black History
Doesn't begin or end
With February
Rather it lives on

In film
In books
In conversations
In memory
Black History is......
Never ending!

Death of the REAL Conversation

Hey sexy
Can I get your name and number?
I wonder
Who's your cell phone provider?
Do you have unlimited text messages?
Do you have a Facebook or MySpace page?
Can I look you up?
Please say yes
This way we can chat for days

Do you IM?
I hope that's not too many questions
1:15 text message
Hey Boo, what are you up to?
1:17 text message
I looked you up on Facebook
But couldn't find you
How do you spell your name again?
Oh okay, I've found you
Picture comment
Picture comment
Picture comment
Wall-to-Wall conversation
Message about your status
This is how it begins
Death of the REAL conversation

We can live in the same city

On the same block
But we can't stop
To carry on real conversations
We've become a nation
Of text messages, status comments and IM's
Too lazy to pick up the phone
Or sit face-to-face
To talk to her or him
Too lazy to build on that bond
So we correspond
Through emails
And web pages
This is the stage
Where conversations are played out

We search our brains
Trying to remember
What your voice sounds like
How deep your thoughts really run
How you keep eye contact
While u-n-i-verse
Instead
We sit in darkness
Our minds void of human contact
We lack
Intimacy
Intensity
They've been replaced
By distance
Increasing the void
As we avoid
Face-to-face interaction
Can't even build on this attraction
Because computers and cell phones
Have become a huge distraction

We'd rather sit and text for hours
Fingers numb
Hearts empty
Souls longing
For some simple human relation
Needing the joy of laughter
Laced with real conversation
Needing to express pain
Laced with real conversation
Needing to connect
With something other than a keyboard
Needing to hear
The realness in your voice
To feel normal again

But this has become
So passé
We spend our days
Neglecting
Real conversation

Forgetting how liberating
It is
When u-n-i-verse
Conversation is dead
Being loaded up
In its hearse
On its way to be
Eulogized
And put to rest
The fight within conversation died
As we constantly set it aside
Too busy
To go back to the old school
When conversing for hours
Was cool

We destroyed its elation
Took away its salvation
Replaced all that
With sub-human conversation
Pushed it aside
Until it slowly died
From frustration
With the creation of
Cyber conversations

No longer
Do we know how
To connect on a normal level
No longer
Do we know
The beauty of verbally exchanging words
No longer
Do we know
The importance of face-to-face communication
Wish this was just a dream
Or that it was just on vacation
Coming back to rescue us
From this damnation
But as technology moves forward
We'll continue to endure
The death of REAL conversation!

Epiphany Bound

Profound
Simply put
Your personality has me
Spellbound

I've explored
The emotional depths of you
Like a dream come true
You appeared
When my soul was achin'
Stopped my heart from breakin'

Brought me back into the light
When all seemed wrong
You showed me what was right
Took me by the mind
Opened my third eye
So now I am no longer blind

Epiphany bound
You are my degree
From the college of life
Pursuin you like knowledge
So I can be your future wife

I professed to you my goal
Got my life under control
Not sailin' aimlessly

Through the sea of life
I've got purpose now
'Cause someway somehow
My life's plan is gonna go down

Willingly
I've given myself to you
With untainted eyes
I see the beauty in you

A King in his own rite
Spiritually you brought me out of darkness
I see things clearly
Now they shine so brightly
So nightly
I find myself thankful
No longer regretful

My heart is open wide
So come on inside
Dwell in the very best of me
It's destiny
That we live on for infinity
In a bond
Created between you and me
Just waitin on you
To turn this possibility
Into a reality

Wise words spoken
From your future Earth
Waitin to birth
A new breed
From your seed
This is not a want
Rather a need

To connect
With a true King
This more than a fling
It's a proclamation
Of my dedication
To you

Epiphany bound
You are my degree
From the college of life
Pursuin you like knowledge
So that I can be your future wife

I hate that I love you

Caught by a spell he cast
Like a spiders web, getting out proves useless to me, his prey
Unknowingly, he draws me in
Not with deceit, but by being himself
The epitome of a man
A sexual God
A spiritual King
An emotional Guardian
A divine physical specimen
His smile breaks down any walls I've built
His eyes, so beautiful and brown, pierce my soul
He
He makes me weak beyond belief

I tried to fight this feeling
I tried to keep my emotional distance
But I have failed
I don't want to love him
But I can't fight it
I don't want to need him
But I can't help it

He exudes beauty
With his words
With his supreme mentality
With his touch
With his kiss

I don't want to love him
But I don't want anyone but him
I try to erase him from my memory's rolodex
But visions of him play on in my mind like a feature
    presentation
I try to cut my love for him from my heart
But his voice is like a suture, piecing my heart back together
    again

I want to forget his touch
But I can taste him in my dreams
I want to forget his smell
But his scent is etched in my soul

I hate that I love him
But I don't know what to do without him
I am convinced that one day he will be mine
But reality shows me that what I want, will never be

He is so perfect
It's like my wants and desires
Were dissected into ingredients
And mixed together to form Him

I try to pretend
That I am okay with our present situation
But this situation dictates that I accept
What I've come to regret
Being in love
With someone who only wants to be friends
So I pretend
That I can maintain
So I remain
Torn
I try to accept, instead of regret
So I can keep him in my life

My end goal has been thwarted
Before it could even begin
I can only be his friend
And not eventually his wife

Torn
Like pieces of paper
I try to rearrange each piece
To fit differently
So the outcome
Is more bearable
Not comparable
To the pain I feel
Each time I make myself face this reality
Not the fallacy
I see in my mind
That in time
He will want me

I don't want to love him anymore
But somehow I end up loving him more
I don't want to need him again
But somehow he's there when I need a friend

I hate that I can't get him out of my mind
I hate that I believe all he needs is time
I hate that he is so perfect for me
I hate that even as a friend, he fulfills my needs
I hate that he is so beautiful to me
I hate that his beauty is more than physically

I wish that I could dissect the part of my brain
Where his image dwells
Then maybe I wouldn't feel like
I'm constantly living in Hell

Tell me
Tell me what I can do to hate you
Tell me what I can do
To keep you off my mind
Tell me what I can do
To forget all the wonderful things you are to me
Tell me what I can do
To no longer love you
Tell me what I can do
To no longer want you
Tell me how to forget
How to forget the beautiful images
I have of us making untamable love
Tell me what to do
Tell me how not to love you anymore

12 months of learning you
12 months of wanting you
12 months of needing you
12 months of seeing the beauty in you
12 months is a long time
For someone to make such an impression
In someone else's mind
I try to cry
Hoping my memories of you
Will be washed out with each tear
But the more I cry
The closer I draw your image near
I am at my wits end
I am in love with a man
Who only wants to be my friend

My Heart
Ode to Barbara L. Hughes

To call you an Angel
Is truly an understatement
To call you a Saint
Does you no justice
To call you Grandmother
That is a name that fits you to a tee

You made being a Grandmother
Look as easy as breathing
You made the name Grandmother
Sound as beautiful as a symphony
You were the essence
Of what a Grandmother should be

Loving
Kind
Gentle
Understanding
Forgiving
Spiritual
And firm

These are the qualities
My Grandmother embodied
Loving
She loved us enough
To encourage when needed

And scold when deserved
Kind
She was kind enough
To give you what you wanted
Even if it's not what you really needed
Gentle
She was gentle enough
To treat you better
Than what you may have deserved
Understanding

She was understanding enough
To know that we are not perfect
And not hold that against us
Forgiving
She was forgiving enough
To overlook our flaws
Even if we did things she didn't approve of
Spiritual
She was spiritual enough
To guide us with scripture
To keep us mentally grounded
And firm
She was firm enough
To let us know
When she was displeased with our actions
And firm enough
For us to know
Not to make that mistake again

My Grandmother
Possessed the power
To make you see the good in you
But it was on us
To live up to that expectation

My Grandmother
Taught me strength
Humility
Respect and
Always
Always
Gave me good advice
Let me know she loved me
And kept my eyes on the Lord

She was and still is my heart
I could always hear her advice
Even when we were apart
She helped instill values in me
Grandmother,
I hope I am all you ever wanted me to be

I am sad that He sent His angels
To bring you home
But I know your pain has ended

And spiritually, you'll never leave me alone

He crafted perfection
When He created you
He gave the Hughes family
Someone who was like no other
He gave us Barbara Lee Hughes
Our
Grandmother

My Revolution will be Televised

Today
Today is the day
For some retribution
As I begin my revolution

You see
My revolution will be televised
Not to take anyone by surprise
But so society
Can finally open its eyes

We are so disillusioned
By all this mass confusion
That we can't focus
We've got on blinders
Living in a fantasy land

We're so busy focusin' on
Things that have no meanin'
Like which celebrity
Is sleepin with whomever
Or which celebrity
Has stopped eatin'

We're so worried about
Which NBA team
Is going to the playoffs
Or which entertainer

Got caught
Doing drugs
Cheatin' on their spouse
Or who just bought a five million dollar house

So America
Needs my revolution
To be televised
'Cause our thoughts
Need to be revised
We need to
Exercise our third eye

Become ultimately wise
To see past
The nonsense comin our way
As society preys
On our uniformed state
They contemplate
Our demise
As gas prices continue to rise
As the cost of food
Continues to rise
As the cost of travel
Continues to rise
As the basic cost of livin'
Continues to rise

Yet oil CEO's
Profits are in the billions
And we can't even
Properly educate our children
Foreclosures continue to plague our nation
While the typical American family
Is faced with frustration

So my revolution will be televised
Until society regains its way
Until baby daddies stop going astray
Until women realize their worth
Until young girls stop givin birth
Until "Happiness" is the American dream
Until society stops focusin on C.R.E.A.M

So my revolution will be televised
Until men realize your happiness
Does not lie between our thighs
Until women stop looking for a free meal
Until people learn to always be real and
Until victims of senseless crimes start to heal
Until abused children no longer have to hide their cries
My revolution will be televised!

Only for You

Sweet simplistic love
I'd like for us to share
Monday through Sunday
I'd like to take you there

I see your smile
And it warms me to my core
Drawing me in closer
Making me
Want you more

I look into your eyes
And I can see
The beauty that lies within
I want you as my lover
Not just as my friend

I want to experience
A love that transcends time
We'll travel back and forth
Between here
And the Renaissance time
When love was blooming
And roamed free
In your arms
I will die with thee

Not in the sense

That we are no longer here
But in the climatic sense
So let's die together
My dear

Let's experience a love
That has me speaking in foreign tongues
Let's explore where this takes us
We've only just begun
A romantic love
As we lay beneath the stars
Voulez-vous coucher avec moi ce soir?

Gazing deep into your eyes
I repeat my beautiful request
Voulez-vous coucher avec moi ce soir?
Voulez-vous
Voulez-vous coucher
Avec moi
Avec moi
Ce soir?
Gently rubbing my hands
Across your bare chest
My heart is racing
Again I repeat my request
Voulez-vous coucher avec moi ce soir?
Voulez-vous
Voulez-vous coucher
Avec moi
Avec moi
Ce soir?

Only for you
Will I offer up the best of me
Infinity
Knows no time limits

As we've only just begun
So who knows when we'll finish

Laying beneath the stars
I again whisper softly
Voulez-vous coucher avec moi ce soir?
Voulez-vous
Voulez-vous coucher
Avec moi
Avec moi
Ce soir?

You give me my answer
Without words
Letting your actions
Speak to my soul
Tappin' into my emotions
I've lost all control
Sweet
Simple
Pleasure
Of knowing

We've tapped into each others minds
Now,
We can go on pleasing one another
Time
After
Time

Passionate
Each time we meet
Seductive
Each time we become one
Blissful
So, blissful

I always begin to cry
When I'm with you
I always die
You are my fantasies come true
Dying is something
I only do
For you

She

She
She is a woman
Who knows where
Her beauty lies

She
She is defined
By more than
How she looks
By more than
How thick she is
By more than
How full her lips are
By more than
The color of her eyes
By more than
The curvature of her body

Her measurements
Are not always
36-24-36
But she has beautiful curves
Nonetheless

She
She refuses to be labeled
She refuses to submit
To one Genre

One Faith
One Category

She
She is above being petty
She is above "he said she said"
She is above drama
She is above ignorance
She is above playing games
She is focused
Focused on being a better She
Focused on building a happy home
Focused on her family
Her friends
Her future

She
She has always
Taken the road less traveled
She has always
Done the unthinkable
Even when others
Told her it was impossible

She
She is more beautiful
Than any woman on TV
She is sexier
Than any lingerie model
She is more sensual
Than any woman you could imagine

She
She exudes beauty
She embodies sensuality
She has mastered being sexy

Her beauty comes from
The love she gives her man
Her sensuality comes from
The home cooked meals she prepares
She is sexy
Even while carrying your love child

She
She knows
There is nothing more beautiful
Than a woman
Who is down for you
Than a woman
Who has your favorite drink waiting for you
When you get home
Than a woman
Who is real with you
And you can be real with her

She
She knows
There is nothing more sensual
Than her in the kitchen
Cooking up some collard greens
Fried chicken
And corn bread
Oh but wait
She also makes
Some mean lasagna
Some fierce enchiladas
And some slap yo momma
'Cause it's so good
Jerk chicken
She knows
How to work her magic

So her man is satisfied
She always
Leaves your mouth watering

She
She knows
There is nothing sexier
Than a woman's glow
From carrying your love-child
Than a woman birthing your seed
Sealing your bond

She
She has birthed
Kings, queens and martyrs
From her womb
Life begins and ends
With her

She
She is stripped of labels
Stripped of false judgment
Stripped of grudges
Stripped of lies
Stripped of hate
She is stripped bare

She
She is more than
Her skin tone
She is more than
How she fills out a shirt or some jeans
She is more than intimate pleasure
She is an epiphany
Waiting for you to embrace
She is euphoric

Once you get to know her
She is pure
She is real
Touch her mentally
Caress her spiritually
Love her physically
'Cause she is waiting

Open your eyes
Wipe the sleep away
Take off your blinders
And behold
She

Single with Purpose

My status
I'm single with purpose
As I walk this earth's surface
I've got my mind set on you
Just waitin' on you
To make my dreams come true

You are a want and a need
I use you to feed
My soul
Help me stay in control
Of my life
My hopes
And my dreams
Life use to be difficult
But thanks to you
Things seem
More bearable
Pleasurable
I can't wait to spend my life with you
You
Enlightened my mind
Took the time
To get to know me
In all my complexities
Showed me the beauty
I forgot was in me

My status
Single with purpose
As I walk this earth's surface
I'm focused on a King
Who embodies everything
I've been searchin' for
You're the one I truly adore
You've touched my soul
Fed my mind
Nourished my body
You complete me
You are my hopes and my dreams

Transformed into a man
So let me do all that I can
To keep a smile on your face
Embrace
This love that's waitin' for you
You're a fixture in my life
That can't be replaced
Erased from my mind
Your image stands the test of time
Now I'm just waitin
Waitin for you to be mine

I live, sleep, eat and breathe you
A feelin' so strong
There's no way it can be misconstrued
Waitin' to start life anew
With you
Debut together
As husband and wife
Rather King and Queen
Intertwined by our minds
United
Never to be divided

By mere mortals
Or drama
I'm gonna
Hold you down
'Til death do us part
Even then
You'll live on in my heart

So I've confessed to you
What I want from you
Just know that for you
I'll continue to wait
This is fate
That we end up together
Through any kind of weather
Just waitin' on you
My King,
To crown your Queen
So until then
While I walk this earth's surface
My status will remain
Single with purpose

Beautiful Are We

Beautiful are we
Dancing tribal dances
In our native land
Beautiful are we
Sitting on thrones as
Kings and Queens

Beautiful are we
Surviving the unthinkable
Persevering through slavery
Hatred and
Racism

Beautiful are we
Providing contributions
To the greatest nation
Inventions born from
Once enslaved minds

Beautiful are we
Standing in solidarity
Beautiful are we
Sacrificing ourselves
For the greater good
Of all mankind

Beautiful are we
Generals

Colonels
Chiefs
Judges
Doctors
Lawyers
Beautiful are we
Leading our youth
Away from the dark
And into the light

Beautiful are we
From our past
To our present
From Africa
To America
Beautiful are we
Beautiful are we

Beautiful are we
Enriching our country
Educating our youth
Emancipating troubled souls
Helping provide hope
To the weary
Hope to the tired
Hope to the lost
Hope to the hurting

Beautiful are we
Commanding respect
Demanding equality
Understanding unity
Expanding our horizons
On the continued growth
Of this great nation

Beautiful are we
Beautiful are we
Beautiful are We

Waiting for You

Perfection
Perfection seems so far fetched
But coming close
Is easy
We all seek perfection
In many different areas in our lives
Our looks
Our wealth and
Our relationships

It almost seems
Next to impossible
To find that perfect someone
But if you wait......
You will find someone
Who is as close to perfection
As you can get

Perfection in a mate
Is not based on
Physical appearances
How much money they make
Rather
The bond you build
What you learn from each other
What you teach each other
How you communicate
On a spiritual level

Emotional level
And sexual level

Can you communicate
Your spiritual beliefs
And be understanding of theirs
Can you communicate
Your emotions
And except theirs
Can you communicate
Your sexual needs
And embrace theirs

If you find someone
With whom you can grow together with
And still be okay with giving them their space
If you find someone
With whom you can explore religions
And find a common ground in your respective religions
If you find someone
You can be open sexually with
And continue to challenge each other's sexual limits
Then you have found your version of perfection

That's what I've found
That's what I've been searching for
Someone whose mind
Continually invites me to explore it
Someone whose beliefs
I can relate to and appreciate
Someone who challenges my mentals
Someone who keeps me grounded and sane
Someone who pushes me to be a better me
Someone who's physically perfect
Sexually amazing
And just overall

Beautiful

I understand
That he has his ups and downs
That he has mood swings just like anyone else
But that's part of life
Taking the good with the bad
So, for him
I'll wait
I'll wait
Because though he's not perfect
He is my idea of perfection
He is my idea of what a man should be
So, for him
I'll wait

Tuskegee Airmen

Take a journey with me
Back in history
To the early 1940's
To a time when racism and hate
Flourished freely
Where we were still fighting for equality

Take a journey with me
To a time when this country
Was at war
And black men answered that call
Stood tall
Ready to serve
A nation
That constantly showed them discrimination

Yet they pursued their dream
Earning their wings
Ready to fight and die
If that was to be their fate
They chose to overcome hate
The great
Tuskegee Airmen
Proved themselves again and again
Overcoming obstacles placed in their way
Without delay
They displayed their skills
Impressive enough for Eleanor Roosevelt

To demand they be allowed to fight
Igniting in them
The spark to continue
With their destiny
Surpassing others scrutiny

The Tuskegee Airmen
Flew some of the greatest missions
Under the harshest conditions
The red-tailed escorts
Made it a point to ensure others safety
Risking their lives
Daily

112 aerial victories
Marked their place in history
Paved the way
For today's African Americans in the military

150 Distinguished Flying Crosses earned
744 Air Medals
8 Purple Hearts and
14 Bronze Stars
Are just a few of their many accomplishments
But to date
They are still
The best the ever did it

So thank you
For making it possible
For me to be where I am today
Thank you
For all you endured and overcame
Thank you
For not losing focus and pursuing your dream
Thank you

And I know if given the opportunity
You'd do it all again
The best that ever did it
The Tuskegee Airmen!

Lost in Euphoria

When I think about you
I feel rejuvenated
I can feel your aura
Covering me
Surrounding me
Protecting me
Your aura
Has me lost in euphoria

This sensation
Of complete elation
Erases all my frustration
Takes me on a mental vacation
Takes me away
From things that stress me
You bring out the very best in me
Even when we disagree
There's a lesson to be learned
To be applied to everyday life
As I understand the knowledge you provide to wise my dome
My soul is firmly planted now
No longer does it roam

Thanks to you
My mind is no longer sedated
My thoughts have been updated
Now
I'm feeling completely elated

I'm blissfully at peace
My past pains have finally ceased
To exist
This is the purist
Happiness
Happier than
I've ever been
And I owe it all to you
My friend
Thanks to your powerful aura
I'm lost in euphoria

I pray this feeling never ends
Each day when I arise
I hope it starts again and again
You don't even have to be near
For me to feel your presence
The essence of you
Shines through
As bright as the sun and the moon
I'm illuminated my you

Mathematically
Our 1+2=3
Keys to life
Our knowledge+wisdom borns understanding
Scientifically proven
So you know this is right
I did the math
Equated you as my better half

You've become my muse
So I use
You to excel
Escape my past hell

I'll continue to dwell
In a much better place
With a smile on my face
I embrace
This feeling
That has surpassed infinity
Sealing this bond
Created by adding your masculinity to my femininity
So I'll keep
Engulfing myself in your aura
Happily
I'm lost in euphoria

About the Author

Dawn L. Douglas, who goes by the moniker Soul Food Poems, was born and raised in Louisville, KY. She left home January 1994 to join the Air Force, where she has proudly served the last 19 years. Poetry is not only her passion, but has become a huge part of who she is, what she does and how she gives back to those she encounters.